SOVIET POEMS

Acknowledgment:

The Kobzar appeared in *Contemporary Verse Two*

Photo : on title page — Ralph Gustafson in Sovietskaya Hotel, Moscow, Sept. 17, 1976.

SOVJET POEMS

Sept. 13 to Oct. 5, 1976

by Ralph Gustafson

Turnstone Press

Ralph Gustafson, who was born and raised in the Eastern Townships area of Quebec, has published numerous books of poems, including *Fire on Stone* for which he received the Governor General's Award in 1974. He has taught English and is Poet-in-Residence at Bishop's University in Lennoxville, Quebec.

hardcover ISBN 0-88801-010-9
softcover ISBN No. 0-8801-008-7

Contents

SOVIET POEMS

This was a journey to the Union of Soviet Socialist Republics under the aegis of the Canadian Department of External Affairs in treaty with the Kremlin. The administrative details of the Programme state that the two countries "agree to exchange on the basis of mutual interest, two writers or poets (sic) to make contacts and familiarize themselves with the other country." Its burden assigned to poets, the purpose becomes humanness recovered, prejudice erased, misconception dismissed; a voyage of individuals whose concern is nothing but the transportation of truth.

The present voyage resulted in nineteen poems in twenty-one days, the two end-days in the air between Montreal and Moscow being concerned with legs.

What looked like poems were written down off the cuff, some on pieces of paper the wrong shape for the poem. Representatives of the Soviet Writers Union, vodka and caviar, were protocol. Al Purdy was companion; Betty and Eurithe, indispensable.

That first night on Red Square in Moscow strange history, future and past, was touched: an eloquence of cobbles; St. Basil's, the intricate cathedral, not to be duplicated, the eyes of its architects put out by Ivan the Terrible, and though now without God, social realism being atheist, beautiful, 'krasnaya' in the 17th century meaning 'beautiful' and now meaning 'red'; the great stretch of the Square edged by the Kremlin wall holding the ashes of its famous men, Lenin lying in his mausoleum beside it:

RED SQUARE

A half moon with a star above it,
Silver, just upward of the moon
When it should be below, the star as usual;
Both above the citadel, the kremlin
Wall silent where the heroes
Are, ashes who made the great square
Red, *krasnaya*, where Lenin lies.
Moonlight floods the Square. We
Before Saint Basil's, God gone,
Between the grounded mind and what it
Wills, intercession not needed.
Faithful, Basil's clustered churches,
The nine, nestled in their past,
Domes and towers, twisted blue
And gold, knotted crimson washed
By the servile moon, intuitive cleave
And clearance, one articulation
Only, as they who built it blinded
So there could not be another.
Beauty not to be commanded,
Or tomb or hero not to be,
Briefness fulfilled as we stand here.

The next day I saw the woman with her twig broom sweeping Kuibysheva Street, off Red Square, alongside the traffic and commercialism of the great GUM, the state department store where double queues each a block long wait inside to buy a pair of shoes:

THE OLD MOSCOW WOMAN

The woman this morning sweeps the pavement
Of Kuibysheva Street,
Branches of spring tied to an old stick,
Brushing along last night's bits
Of paper, cigarette ends, dirt,
Keeping the city clean for this morning's
Traffic. By night it will have to be done
All over again. She looks happy.
What is this happiness? Grandchildren,
Soup on the stove, an hour's relief
From pain, Lenin sleeping nearby?
The street will always be dirty.
Mankind is imperfect.
Politics and bad manners
Leave his detritus
On the perfect peace. We
Do not understand one another.
The street will have to be swept again.
New York, Moscow, Montreal,
It is the same. Man is careless,
He drops the wrappings from his hands,
The torn paper, even the newspaper
With the news of the world
He leaves behind him to be picked up
By someone else. The wind is cold.
This is September. Soon the snow
Will cover the shivering gutter
And the plough will supersede the broom.
We all feel it. No matter the labour.
Snow and death come.
Do they not?
And yet this woman sweeps,
For a few kopeks,
Lentils for her soup,
And is happy.
What is this Moscow?
This humanity?

And then, on Gorky Street, I saw the gun in the yard of the Museum of the Revolution, used by the troops to fire on the Kremlin in October 1917. Put into my head were lines from Alexander Blok's poem, "The Twelve": the old weeping woman who doesn't know what the political banner hung across the street is about, but thinks how many leggings it would make for cold children:

MEMORIAL GUN ON GORKY STREET
(on a line in Blok's poem, "The Twelve")

Like the old crone and the political banner
From house to house across the street
Whose cloth otherwise
Could keep children warm,
I look at the military hardware
Monumental in the plaza.
I am reminded of other hardware
In the arms of girls,
Rusted irony.
The detonator won't pull,
The screw accomodation is
Too worn for firing.
The old crone is right.
A pair of scissors,
Expenditure cut down
Might scare up some money for
A few orange lollipops for the children.
Happiness is not hard to come by,
It is not expensive.
What of the filing-cabinets, you say?
The erasers and
Duplicate copies?
Where would the papers be
Not in alphabetical order?
Responses would falter,
Accords would fail.
Turn banners into baby-linen,
Balances of advantage,
Peace, would disappear.
What of the chocolates for the children?

We went to the Moscow circus. But it was not to the old one our translator took us — the one with the bears, the clowns — but to the new circus with the chromium and the spangles. The West has to be shown. Never mind. I used the cliché — the world a circus, one mistake and — zap! that's it:

MOSCOW CIRCUS

Hung by wire. Four and four
(The figure Jung said expressed
The ultimate divine reality within us)
The figures of the four girls,
The four guys, spangled,
Walking the tightrope,
Flaw each side of them across
The tent top, birth to death,
Equilibrist, each toe delicate
Set in front, Natasha upside down
On Vasily's head. Strobe
Lights play, drum
Points, the whole Copernicus put
On a step . . . She's pretty. He,
Axiom. They reach the platform,
Whirl, salute the world.
Next time, next time:
Misunderstanding,
Slackened love . . .

With required earnestness, that Thursday, we went to Tolstoy's home, 125 miles outside of Moscow, to the south . . . Only the party bosses, the 'nachalstvo,' ride in chauffeur-driven limousines. An unheard-of thing happened to Canadian poetry:

THE RIDE TO YASNAYA POLYANA

Past the birches,
Across the Oka.
Beyond the Moscow Region,
Into Tula, the country
Began to roll. We drew up
At the roadside. Moles,
Mushroom spotted scarlet,
Sky and pine trees —
Cheese and sausage washed down
With pop. Parked,
The *Chaika* sat, "Seagull",
Sweet sixteen, once owned
By Tereshkova, female
First in silent
Space. Got going,
Down the centre,
By cow nor crossroad
Slowed nor swerved,
Trucks to hub of us,
Zaporozhets, left,
Putt and thunder,
Bystander, apparatchik, sentry,
Saluted, blurred,
Communist nobility only
So richly conveyed.

Bardship Kanuckski
Never so bowed to,
Erroneously erred to,
Stanza and senza,
Purdy, Gustafson,
Never so mutely,
Astutely proclaimed.

At Tolstoy's house we learned much, of contradictions. My father when he first, as a young man, came to Canada from Sweden, wore kid gloves to pile cordwood. That was out of dignity. Tolstoy ploughed, mowed, sawed wood, without any such thought. Just the same . . .

TOLSTOY'S ESTATE

Of accommodations there is no end:
Tolstoy who laboured in the field with the peasants,
The footman at his door:
"Master, the plough is ready."

*I had replied Samarkand without hesita-
tion when asked, in Canada, where I would
like to go. I was naming romance: Central
Asia, caravans from the East, the tomb of
Tamerlane. By Aeroflot from Moscow we
flew to Uzbekistan . . .*

*. . . stood there, that first night, in front of
Samarkand's Schools, the great 'madrasahs'
where Ulugh Beg, astronomer of the 15th
century, taught the sacred laws — his
courtyards now only a destination for tourists
in the undeified town. Yet, as I turned in the
dark, there were the two old men, their hands
lifted in amen to their prayers:*

NIGHT, SAMARKAND

We flew with the sun into the sun
Lying low on the wide horizon
Like a disc of copper metal
Thrown by luck. Later, the moon,
Half itself, washed silver the walls
Of the sapphire Schools where silence
Is, blue, glazed, across
The court, the leaning minaret;
Each side, archways, glossed,
Majolica, comb and scripted gold
The inner traves, portals portioned
As the milky way, that looked on
Present brick. We stood in the shadow.
The dog beside the broken pavement
Scratched fleas, sloped poles
Brought wire to the flooding lights.
Starry with history, Ulugh Beg.
I turned. The night was cold. The two
Old men, in moonlight, touched their foreheads,
Prayer done, shifting, marking,
The future of the hopeful past.

Romance gives way: Theseus walked out of his labyrinth because he had his feet on the ground; Icarus flew too near the sun. In Samarkand, once lived Bibi the beloved of Timur the Magnificent. Not long ago, they excavated on his practical hill Ulugh Beg's mammoth quadrant for the mathematical stars:

STARDUST AND QUADRANT

Of the tumbled stone, an archway,
Tilted minaret, remain . . .
Lovely she was, of all of China, who loved
Timur the Lame, Bibi Khanum left
Behind while to compensate his short foot
Timur conquered Persia, the ruby Ind.
The pomegranate ripened. Sick with love,
She ordered court and school of fabulous measure
Raised to him. The great arch grew.
Magnificent the furnaces, the glazing tile,
Entablature, ranked by scaffold to
The rising sun. No more. Work stopped.
Morning stained the tiles. Ragged the wall,
The architect in love. The stork set down
His nest. Bibi pleaded. Still, mihrab,
Honeycomb and dome, magnificent utmost
Unfulfilled, the builder refused till she
Had let him kiss her cheek. She thought of
Starry parapet and Tamerlane. The kiss
Burned through her hand raised to shield it,
Left the imprint of his lips. Ill-timed,
Tamerlane's return. From top to bottom,
Thrown from minaret, past onyx, turquoise,
The lover fell. Splat.
So goes the story.

Sighting his practical quadrant, his grandmother Bibi
Sucking porridge, Ulugh Beg
Cradles the stars.

In the modern town of Tashkent is a crossroads, once those of the fabled caravans from the East. In the pathway now stands the State Department Store, known in the Soviet Republics by the initials G.U.M.:

TASHKENT

Banish the camel if there ever was one,
Speak of Marx and GUM.
There the crossroads were,
Shangtu to Hormuz, Canton
To Trebizond, Gobi
Lifted by hoofprints bringing
Sandsick aromatics, nutten hot spices
Richer than ruby
For mention in Chaucer's hand.
Here, transistors, card and tin.

Bearing silk and sandril
Up Rustaveli Prospekt
Goes the ghostly caravan
Through impermeable GUM.

From Tashkent to Kiev in the Ukraine. At Kiev, offices at The Whole World magazine; on foot through the park above the Dnieper; to the churches and monasteries of the middle ages, intact, in metaphorical ruin:

THE CHURCHES OF KIEV

1. IN THE MONASTERY OF THE CAVES

Walled up for God underground,
Bricked in alive, tomb
On tomb, labyrinth
Safe from the world. *O dies irae*!
Assumption of the crown of thorns!

o exit. Bleeding hearts,
Entombment done with.
Outside again, my love,
"The song?" she said.
"Hear it? The bird?"

2. MOSAICS AT ST. SOPHIA

A slightly walleyed Virgin Mary,
A handkerchief in her belt.
Well, she can have hay-fever, can't she,
Unable to wear contact lens?
We have our computers,
The Artificial Intelligence Laboratory
At Stanford University
My friend is at. Do we
Need natural faith? *Ichthys*,
Worship of a fish?
Do we need that?
Of course not. Xerox reigns.
So then, let Mary be walleyed
In a squinch of gold,
As valid, up into heaven
Uncorrupt like an
Otis elevator.

3. ST. CYRIL'S, 12th CENTURY

What wonders cease when we are
Casual and indifferent
To simple faith.

I climb the church stairs
Within the crude wall
And come on God

In the likeness of others' love,
Arches bend roughly coloured
With ancient saints.

Nonsense, I say, a waste
Of emotion and hurt and
Grief unanswered.

I am rebuked. What comfort
Of theirs do I know of?
What crying ceased?

I wander the balcony of
The church with my faith
In nothing and poems.

I see the end of arrogance,
On the walls, trumpets sound,
The angel rolls up the sky.

And during that tour of Kiev, the silencing, at Babiy Yar, the ravine in the environs where 96,000 Jews were slaughtered and piled under by the Nazis. A great bronze memorial has been erected on the spot. Nowhere are the Jews mentioned:

AT BABIY YAR

Yevtushenko, that line of yours,
'Over Babiy Yar there are no memorials.'
Now this monument turns your words to bronze.

Still the earth pulses with the movements of the dead
Not dead, dying of our guilt who do not
Supersede the brute.

      What command?
Lie peacefully at rest? We shall remember?

Nothing but silence and the silent
Wording of the heart.

Dictatorship dislikes poets. Their words are stronger than tyranny. Taras Shevchenko, in 1847, was kept in Orsk Fortress; was exiled to the Caspian Sea. Kobzars in the Ukraine still sing his poems of freedom to the music of their stringed instrument, the kobza:

THE KOBZAR

Shevchenko, searched
For bits of paper,
Incendiary poems
On them, by police
On his Caspian isle,
Verses of Morintsi,
Poltava, lines
Of fire, a Czardom
Less than words,
Russia trembled,
The loud world
Shook; frisked
For scraps of words,
The poet, sick
In exile, no use
To anyone but
His bits of paper
And the listening world.
Pound in Pisa,
Without paper, shade
Or hat, yet
The poems, cantos
Canting the world.
Shevchenko, serf;
Ezra, apostle
Of Benno: uncomparable,
Yet the poem;
Cancer in the belly

And Solzhenitsyn;
Wagner fleeing
Dresden, his grenade
Cocked for liberty,
But tossed for himself,
Freeloader, pander,
Yet the music;
Exiled, Dante,
Ovid; Lorca
Full of lead.
Paper persists.
Poetry "makes nothing
Happen. A mouth."
Auden, rewrite:
They read Shevchenko
In the Ukraine!

Shadows gather
Under the linden
Where he sat
In Kiev; red
October. Acorns
Fall. On the Dnieper
It's cold. I think
Of tyrannies; the kobza.
In the fields of enmity
Syllables survive.

*From Kiev, the flight to Riga in Latvia; of
mighty matters, to that which matters:*

WINGED FLIGHT

The half moon on the plane wing
Gilded the flight; Kiev, all
The Urals to the plains, Bukhara
To emerald Shakhi-Zinda, behind us.
The Caspian, Shevchenko exiled, a silver
Wedge. Beyond: the Baltic. Easy,
Sweden, come-to— that summer remembered,
Juno nightly churning, slow,
Through Vänern where the new moon lay
On waters of the north. Remote,
The moon, enough to bind the world,
Samarkand to golden Colchis,
Back to Massawippi where
The Argo lies. Lies! No sooner,
Than the truth: all of Mercator,
Marx and dialectic; dinner,
Aeroflot's chicken hunked and cut,
Entrails sliced in profile; poems,
Plane and Russia; Växjö, the earth
Of Tashkent shaken — nothing, not a worth,
Against the profile of (as Eden
To Satan's tilted flight) her nose.

Of all the met poets and prosers, not a word from them of music:

IN PHILHARMONIC HALL, RIGA

Out of harmony, out of music, is poetry.
Ferruccio Busoni. Ask. Not
A wordsmith's heard of him. Riga, two
Descendants from him who after Liszt, shook
The piano world, faced Faust here.
Poets have moved from soundings. Bleak rhythms!
Dowland, Milton, Browning, Pound in
Their major graves. Minor resurrections
Deaf as hammered door-nails. What they say,
Tyrannical to how it's done. Consider this hall
Not a pindrop, listening, where Wagner fled to,
Busoni came; respecting the greater art.

At Jurmala the Baltic tide was ebbed. That night, we searched out music in Riga. St. Mary's cathedral was crowded:

IN THE CATHEDRAL

On the pulpit, mounting its stairs:
The martyrs carved in gilt
Wood, rococo each with his
Axe, his saw, all
Subservient to God,
God everywhere
In the Dom, arch and aisle,
In the instructed heart, the listeners
Still, below; organ
Vast with sound, pipes
Vertical to heaven.
O concert in the Dom.
Sweetly Schubert sounds.
Gracious, Handel's pace.
At Jurmala the tide comes in.
For a moment, here,
The purpose of martyrdom.

From Riga by train to Leningrad; from Leningrad by limousine to Novgorod. Thousands of miles anywhere, destination always a house with a lamp. Once, in Sweden, I had written of that, the sudden sanctuary (which is the poem too), of coming home, a lighted window across the snows; so it was now, of the small houses, the 'izbas' of Russia:

ON THE ROAD TO NOVGOROD

Grass white where the shadows are,
On brake and hummock, the forest-road.
The highway to Novgorod. The log
Houses warm. The sun cold.
The birch frosted. At the coppice edge,
Potatoes harvested, bent red
The women's kerchiefs, a hundred along
The field-rows; in the pickup, melons
From Tashkent, on the road-warning,
Running children from anywhere.
While we pass, the old woman
Interrupts her cow, the hunch
Of ground starlings takes off.

And coming home, crimson dusk,
At the edge of the distant woods a house,
Smoke from the chimney, a lighted room.

Deified and guarded, Lenin lies in his mausoleum on Red Square. The queue that October Sunday stretched forever:

THE SKULL BENEATH THE SKIN

I saw one thousand nine hundred and seventy-six
People waiting to get into Lenin's tomb,
Tartar, Russian, Uzbek, Kasakh and
Canadian, some carrying purses,
Some, cameras, some wore kerchiefs,
Some inhabited uniforms, I saw children,
The wise, those once-suffered, the old, each
In line, moved slowly, moving between
White lines drawn on the pavement
To get into the tomb, one thousand
Nine hundred and seventy-six, one thousand
Nine hundred and seventy-six skulls.

We come to conclusions. Unpolitical humanity is the same. I stood again on Red Square, the night before coming home, to Canada: St. Basil's before me under the same moon, to the left the round platform, Lobnoye Mesto, 'The Place of the Forehead', where imperial decrees were proclaimed, victims executed, Lenin in his marble mortality behind me:

BY WAY OF POSTLUDE

Prescriptive optimism in all things,
One gets weary of official virtue,
Pictures of good workers on the wall,
Red Star over the avenues,
Church and danced pin and toothpaste,
Sick of piety always
There first. Where the ease
From branded presumptions of the future, laughter,
The natural factory, the unstatistical labour?
O the heroic statue, the striding
Into the dawn, the sword raised victorious!
O modesty, not higher, not bigger.
Nothing is wrong here liberty
Won't cure.

     And yet,

O Russia, O Uzbekistan and Ukraine,
Latvia. Where more generosity,
Where more honourably glorious dead,
More friendship and giving? The strictures,
They would not come at all if not
From love, I would not write this down
Not aware of freedom's own failures,
The poet not his own revolution.

I stand again in Red Square,
The goose-stepping exact guard gone,
Lenin left alone, the half moon
At eleven, over St. Basil's,
The Place of the Forehead, the round ukase
Empty, the stones of the Square immaculate
With night. My mind fills,
Those three weeks, poems the successors . . .

Quiet with admonitions the time-zones,
The Rockies white with glaciers under
The Moscow moon, these silent bells
Heavy with burdens of Canadian snows.

c. Ralph Gustafson

Turnstone Press

Soviet Poems by Ralph Gustafson

Poetry Series Two
Number Two

An edition of 750 copies, 150 of which are
hardcover, 26 of which are lettered and
signed by the author.

Soviet Poems was set in Univers 11 point
medium, bold and italic.
The cover is Classic Cover Antique Grey,
the text is Classic Natural White, the endpapers
and dustjacket are Classic Baronial Ivory.

The book was designed at Turnstone Press
by Eva Fritsch.

Turnstone Press gratefully acknowledges a
grant from the Canada Council that has
aided in the publication of this book.

TURNSTONE PRESS
St. John's College,
University of Manitoba,
Winnipeg, Canada,
R3T 2M5.

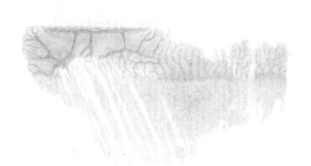